D1385071

MULTIGENERATIONAL FAMILIES

Families Today

Adoptive Families

Disability and Families

Foster Families

Homelessness and Families

Immigrant Families

Incarceration and Families

LGBT Families

Military Families

Multigenerational Families

Multiracial Families

Single-Parent Families

Teen Parents

Families Today

MULTIGENERATIONAL FAMILIES

H.W. Poole

MASON CREST

Mason Crest
450 Parkway Drive, Suite D
Broomall, PA 19008
www.masoncrest.com

MTM Publishing, Inc.
435 West 23rd Street, #8C
New York, NY 10011
www.mtmpublishing.com

President: Valerie Tomaselli
Vice President, Book Development: Hilary Poole
Designer: Annemarie Redmond
Copyeditor: Peter Jaskowiak
Editorial Assistant: Andrea St. Aubin

Series ISBN: 978-1-4222-3612-3
Hardback ISBN: 978-1-4222-3621-5
E-Book ISBN: 978-1-4222-8265-6

Library of Congress Cataloging-in-Publication Data
Names: Poole, Hilary W., author.
Title: Multigenerational families / by H.W. Poole.
Description: Broomall, PA : Mason Crest [2017] | Series: Families Today | Includes index.
Identifiers: LCCN 2016004540| ISBN 9781422236215 (hardback) | ISBN 9781422236123
(series) | ISBN 9781422282656 (e-book)
Subjects: LCSH: Families—Juvenile literature. | Grandparents—Juvenile literature. |
Generations—Juvenile literature.
Classification: LCC HQ744 .P56 2017 | DDC 306.85—dc23
LC record available at http://lccn.loc.gov/2016004540

Printed and bound in the United States of America.

First printing
9 8 7 6 5 4 3 2 1

TABLE OF CONTENTS

Key Icons to Look for:

Words to Understand: These words with their easy-to-understand definitions will increase the reader's understanding of the text, while building vocabulary skills.

Sidebars: This boxed material within the main text allows readers to build knowledge, gain insights, explore possibilities, and broaden their perspectives by weaving together additional information to provide realistic and holistic perspectives.

Research Projects: Readers are pointed toward areas of further inquiry connected to each chapter. Suggestions are provided for projects that encourage deeper research and analysis.

Text-Dependent Questions: These questions send the reader back to the text for more careful attention to the evidence presented there.

Series Glossary of Key Terms: This back-of-the-book glossary contains terminology used throughout the series. Words found here increase the reader's ability to read and comprehend higher-level books and articles in this field.

In the 21st century, families are more diverse than ever before.

SERIES INTRODUCTION

Our vision of "the traditional family" is not nearly as time-honored as one might think. The standard of a mom, a dad, and a couple of kids in a nice house with a white-picket fence is a relic of the 1950s—the heart of the baby boom era. The tumult of the Great Depression followed by a global war caused many Americans to long for safety and predictability—whether such stability was real or not. A newborn mass media was more than happy to serve up this image, in the form of TV shows like *Leave It To Beaver* and *The Adventures of Ozzie and Harriet*. Interestingly, even back in the "glory days" of the traditional family, things were never as simple as they seemed. For example, a number of the classic "traditional" family shows— such as *The Andy Griffith Show, My Three Sons,* and a bit later, *The Courtship of Eddie's Father*—were actually focused on single-parent families.

Sure enough, by the 1960s our image of the "perfect family" was already beginning to fray at the seams. The women's movement, the gay rights movement, and—perhaps more than any single factor—the advent of "no fault" divorce meant that the illusion of the Cleaver family would become harder and harder to maintain. By the early 21st century, only about 7 percent of all family households were traditional—defined as a married couple with children where *only* the father works outside the home.

As the number of these traditional families has declined, "nontraditional" arrangements have increased. There are more single parents, more gay and lesbian parents, and more grandparents raising grandchildren than ever before. Multiracial families—created either through interracial relationships or adoption—are also increasing. Meanwhile, the transition to an all-volunteer military force has meant that there are more kids growing up in military families than there were in the past. Each of these topics is treated in a separate volume in this set.

While some commentators bemoan the decline of the traditional family, others argue that, overall, the recognition of new family arrangements has brought more good than bad. After all, if very few people live like the Cleavers anyway, isn't it better to be honest about that fact? Surely, holding up the traditional family as an ideal to which all should aspire only serves to stigmatize kids whose lives differ from that standard. After all, no children can be held responsible for whatever family they find themselves in; all they can do is grow up as best they can. These books take the position that every family—no matter what it looks like—has the potential to be a successful family.

That being said, challenges and difficulties arise in every family, and nontraditional ones are no exception. For example, single parents tend to be less well off financially than married parents are, and this has long-term impacts on their children. Meanwhile, teenagers who become parents tend to let their educations suffer, which damages their income potential and career possibilities, as well as risking the future educational attainment of their babies. There are some 400,000 children in the foster care system at any given time. We know that the uncertainty of foster care creates real challenges when it comes to both education and emotional health.

Furthermore, some types of "nontraditional" families are ones we wish did not have to exist at all. For example, an estimated 1.6 million children experience homelessness at some point in their lives. At least 40 percent of homeless kids are lesbian, gay, bisexual, or transgender teens who were turned out of their homes because of their orientation. Meanwhile, the United States incarcerates more people than any other nation in the world—about 2.7 million kids (1 in 28) have an incarcerated parent. It would be absurd to pretend that such situations are not extremely stressful and, often, detrimental to kids who have to survive them.

The goal of this set, then, is twofold. First, we've tried to describe the history and shape of various nontraditional families in such a way that kids who aren't familiar with them will be able to not only understand, but empathize. We also present demographic information that may be useful for students who are dipping their toes into introductory sociology concepts.

Second, we have tried to speak specifically to the young people who are living in these nontraditional families. The series strives to address these kids as

Meeting challenges and overcoming them together can make families stronger.

sympathetically and supportively as possible. The volumes look at some of the typical problems that kids in these situations face, and where appropriate, they offer advice and tips for how these kids might get along better in whatever situation confronts them.

Obviously, no single book—whether on disability, the military, divorce, or some other topic—can hope to answer every question or address every problem. To that end, a "Further Reading" section at the back of each book attempts to offer some places to look next. We have also listed appropriate crisis hotlines, for anyone with a need more immediate than can be addressed by a library.

Whether your students have a project to complete or a problem to solve, we hope they will be able to find clear, empathic information about nontraditional families in these pages.

—H. W. Poole

A traditional "nuclear" family has a mother, father, and one or more children.

Chapter One

WHO IS IN A FAMILY?

When politicians and writers talk about the "traditional family," they usually mean one father, one mother, and a few children. Another name for that type of family is a "nuclear" family. According this view, parents and children are the center of society, much like how a **nucleus** is the center of an atom. When people talk about traditional or nuclear families, they sometimes make it sound like humans have always lived that way. Another **implication** is that they *should* always live that way.

Words to Understand

commonwealth: country.

companionate: a relationship of equals that's based on being friends.

implication: something suggested but not said outright.

Industrial Revolution: a period of great social and economic change starting in the late 1700s, when more goods were mass-produced rather than homemade.

nucleus: the center of an atom.

patriarchal: a system that is run by men and fathers.

refuge: a safe place.

Defining the Multigenerational Family

What does the term *multigenerational* really mean? It depends on whom you ask. The strict definition of a multigenerational family is more than two generations of the same family living together. So, if grandparents, parents, and children all live in the same home, that's a multigenerational family with three generations under the same roof. Add great-grandparents, and you have four generations. This is how the U.S. Census Bureau defines the concept of multigenerational family.

However, many social scientists (people who study trends in the way people live) feel that this definition is too limited. These experts say it's important to consider other ways in which different generations can be mixed and matched to create families. So the term multigenerational family is often expanded to mean the following arrangements as well:

- grandparents who live with parents and children ("sandwich" families)
- grandparents who raise their grandchildren without the parents ("skipped generation" families)
- parents with adult children living at home

If you define *multigenerational* in this way, suddenly you're talking about a huge portion of our population: 1 out of 10 kids lives with at least one grandparent.

But history says otherwise. If we look at the history of American families, we see that the "traditional family" has always been changing. For example, families used to live together in much larger groups, with grandparents, parents, and children all pitching in together. We now call this a *multigenerational family*. The size, shape, and nature of families has evolved over the years, and it will continue to evolve in the future.

According to the U.S. Census Bureau, 57 million Americans lived in multigenerational family households in 2012; that's double the number who lived that way in 1980.

A BRIEF HISTORY OF AMERICAN FAMILIES

In the 17th century, families in England and the American colonies were **patriar-chal**, meaning that the father was the boss. The family unit was considered to be a smaller version of the country. In other words, children were supposed to obey their parents in the same way that subjects obeyed the king. For that reason, the family was often called "the little **commonwealth**." The same philosophy that guided politics also guided the family. A lot of marriages were "arranged," meaning that parents decided whom their children should marry.

But as time passed, all this began to change. More people got married for love, rather than because their parents told them to. And because husbands and wives were more likely to choose each other, their relationships slowly began to resemble partnerships, rather than a relationship between king and subject. (This social trend began in the 1800s, but things did not truly change for a long time, until women's rights became an issue in the 20th century.)

Grandparents and grandchildren on a farm in the 1930s.

A replica of a one-room schoolhouse.

The idea of childhood became more important, too. Instead of treating kids as tiny adults, people began to view childhood as a unique and precious time in a person's life. People expressed the view that the home should be a place of love and support. By the 1800s, the family was considered to be a small **refuge** from the outside world, rather than a reflection of it.

Even so, the family had a different social role than it does today. Before there were large-scale stores, families grew or made whatever they needed. Before there were public schools, families educated their own children. Before there were hospitals, families took care of each other when they were sick. Before there were charities and government assistance, families would take in their troubled members. And before there were nursing homes, families looked after elderly members until their lives ended.

The "no-fault" divorce has had a profound effect on our ideas about what makes a family.

Over time, those functions were given to others. For example, work became more specialized. In the past, each family had basically been a self-sustaining unit. After the **Industrial Revolution**, people started focusing on one specific job (weaving, making shoes, or whatever), and then using the money they earned to purchase everything else they needed.

Similarly, kids were sent outside the home to be educated. Initially, schools were run by churches, but gradually local governments began to take over. Meanwhile, people began to trust doctors and hospitals to handle their health care, charities to take care of their poor, and nursing homes to look after their elderly.

What remained was the nuclear family: mom, dad, and kids. Economic progress made it possible for people to marry whom they wanted and when they wanted. They also could live *where* they wanted; people started moving farther away from their families and hometowns. They had fewer children, but they spent more money and attention on the ones they did have. Women increasingly went to work, making time for both career and family. One result of all this social change is a **companionate** family. The companionate family is one that sticks together because they want to, not because they are forced to by law or tradition.

But then something happened. In the 1960s, laws were changed to make divorces easier to get. And we learned that many of those companionate families didn't get along so well, after all.

FRACTURED NUCLEUS

The past 30 years has been an era of great change for the American family. There are lots of reasons for this.

As mentioned above, a trend called "no-fault divorce" meant that people didn't have to stay in bad marriages if they didn't want to. Also, women no longer expected to spend their lives serving a family patriarch; they expected to make their own decisions about how their lives should be. And if they didn't like their lives, women insisted on their right to change things. These days, *both* men and women have higher expectations about being happy than people did years ago.

The economy has shifted from industrial (meaning most jobs involve making things) to postindustrial (meaning most jobs involve services, ideas, or information). A postindustrial economy is great for people who have access to high levels of education, but it presents a huge challenge for people who don't have that access. But even an education is no guarantee of success. Between 2007 and 2009, national unemployment peaked at 10 percent, while in some states (such as California and Michigan), it soared even higher.

Meanwhile, a "war on drugs" has contributed to a huge increase in the number of people in prison. The effect on the American family has been huge: in 2015, 1 in 14 American kids had an incarcerated parent. The United States has also been at war overseas since 2001, and almost 2 million children have at least one parent on active duty with the U.S. military.

There is another important factor to consider. People live a lot longer today than they ever did before. This is obviously a wonderful thing, but it is also challenging for society. How can we best care for the elderly generation, and how will we pay for that care? In the face of change, the American family has adapted yet again.

WHY MULTIGENERATIONAL?

There are a couple of trends that seem to be inspiring the creation of more multigenerational families. One major cause is economics. Often, it just makes more financial sense for families to live together instead of apart. For example, if a grandparent moves in, one less house or apartment has to be paid for. The high cost of housing is frequently mentioned as a major factor in the decision to keep multiple generations under the same roof. Also, grandparents usually help take care of the kids; this can save families huge amounts of money, because child care is so expensive.

There was a sharp spike in multigenerational families during the Great Recession, a worldwide economic slump that occurred between 2007 and 2009. International trade declined while unemployment rose, and the American economy was the worst it had been since the 1930s. Young adults (defined as people between the ages of 25 and 34) began moving back home with their parents in record numbers. By 2012, even though the economy had improved somewhat, 57 million Americans (18.1 percent) were living in multigenerational households. About 25 percent of "young adults" lived in a multigenerational household at that time—up from 18.7 percent when the recession first began in 2007.

More than one-quarter of Asian American families are multigenerational.

During the Great Recession (2007–2009), increasing numbers of young adults found themselves moving back home after college.

Another trend has to do with culture and ethnicity. People who are of Asian, African American, or Hispanic descent are more likely to live in multigenerational families than whites are. For example, 27 percent of Asian Americans live in multigenerational families. That is the highest rate of any ethnicity, although African Americans and people of Hispanic descent are close behind at 25 percent each. By contrast, only 14 percent of white Americans live in multigenerational families.

Interestingly, these percentages have stayed about the same for a very long time. In other words, people of Asian, African, and Hispanic descent have always been more likely to live in multigenerational families. What has changed is that the percentage of nonwhite American families has grown—they were 37 percent of the U.S. population in 2015, up from 20 percent in 1980. So as America becomes less white, it also becomes more multigenerational. According to the Pew Research Center, there are nearly 8 million kids—or 1 in 10—living with at least one grandparent.

Text-Dependent Questions

1. What are some different types of multigenerational families?
2. What are some historical factors that influenced the shape of American families?
3. Which ethnicity is the most likely to live in a multigenerational household?

Research Project

Interview a grandparent or older relative about what his or her childhood was like. Who lived in the house? Who lived nearby? How far away were other relatives? How often did your relative see these more distant relatives, and what did they do together? Answer all these questions yourself, too, and then compare what was alike and what was different for your relative.

An Obama family portrait on Inauguration Day, 2013; Marian Shields Robinson is on the left, in purple.

Chapter Two

SANDWICH FAMILIES

In some ways, Marian Shields Robinson's story is very typical. She was a stay-at-home mom in Chicago, and she and her husband raised two kids, Craig and Michelle. But Marian's life became very unique in 2009. That's when her daughter, now called Michelle Obama, asked Marian to come live in the White House.

When Barack Obama was elected president in 2008, he and Michelle invited Marian to live with them so they could help keep their daughters' lives as normal as possible. For example, for many years, Marian would accompany Sasha and Malia to school every day. Although Marian Robinson lives in one of the most famous homes in the country, she stays out of the public eye and focuses on her grandchildren. "My job here [at the White House] is the easiest one of all," she says, "I just get to be Grandma."

Words to Understand

caregiving: helping someone with their daily activities.

disability: problems with a particular skill; types of disability include sight, hearing, memory, or some physical handicap.

WHAT'S A SANDWICH FAMILY?

The Obamas are probably America's most famous "sandwich" family. The term "sandwich family" was created in 1981 by Dorothy Miller. Miller was writing about adult women who were expected to look after both their parents and their own children. They are, in Miller's view, "sandwiched" between the previous generation and the next one. Today, the term sandwich family is used more broadly for a family that is a "sandwich" of three generations or more.

In 1930 the average life expectancy for an American woman was about 61 years of age, and for a man it was about 58. In 2012 it was 81 years for a woman

People of Hispanic ethnicity are more likely to be supporting multigenerational families than any other ethnicity.

Case Study: Daniel

Daniel lives in a house full of women: his 36-year-old mother, his 77-year-old grandmother, and his 94-year-old great-grandmother. When Daniel was small, Nona, his great-grandmother, was the one who played games with him, sang him songs, and made him laugh. Meanwhile, his grandma was the one who cooked his meals, washed his clothes, scolded him, and put him to bed. Daniel lived in the same house with his mother—but from the time he was born, his grandmother was the one who raised him.

"Nona's so old now, all she does is sleep, and I really miss her," he says. "She was the happy one in our house. Now it seems like my mother and grandma fight all the time." What makes it harder for Daniel is that his mother and grandmother mostly fight about him. His grandmother has lots of experience raising young children, but not much understanding of today's adolescents. So it's no wonder she and her daughter don't agree on how to raise Daniel.

"Grandma was in charge when I was a little kid," Daniel says. "So she thinks she should still be the one who decides what I do and don't do, where I go, what I wear. Now that I'm older, though, my mom wants to be more involved in my life."

One of Daniel's favorite memories is going to a Native American demonstration with his uncle Joey. "One guy said that his people believe that a man who is raised by his mother grows up strong and wise. So I guess I'm going to be double-strong and double-wise when I'm a grownup—because I pretty much have two mothers."

—Adapted from *Grandparents Raising Kids* by Rae Simons (Mason Crest, 2010)

and 76 for a man—a huge increase. As people live longer, more and more adults are pulled in two directions. They are caring for their own children while also caring for aging parents. That can be a lot of responsibility, especially if either the kids or the grandparents have health problems. About 15 percent of people aged 40 to 59 are providing financial support to their aging parents and also supporting at least one of their children. According to the Pew Research Center, that statistic is true across all income groups. However, it is not true across all ethnic groups. In fact, Hispanic families are much more likely to be helping out both generations than any other ethnic group. About 21 percent of Hispanic Americans say that they have financially supported both their parents and their children at some point in the previous year.

Financial support is just one way of caring for someone. A more general term for looking after someone is **caregiving**. About 30 percent of adults say that their aging parents need help taking care of themselves.

MOVING IN

One way that some families make things easier is to gather everybody together under the same roof. These families are the ones who meet the Census Bureau's strict definition of a multigenerational family (see page 12 for more on this issue). The Census Bureau reported that in 2012 there were 4.3 million multigenerational households, or about 5.6 percent of all households in the United States.

Once a family makes the decision to move a grandparent into their home, some interesting challenges arise. Many older people have some type of **disability**. In fact, 25.8 percent of people between the ages of 65 and 74 have a disability, and 50.7 percent of people older than 75 do. If the grandparent who is moving in has a disability, families sometimes need to rearrange or even renovate their homes. Railings or ramps may be needed, for example. There may also be changes to the family schedule. For example, if an elderly person has to take medication at a certain time, mealtimes may be adjusted.

About half of the people over the age of 75 have some form of disability.

Responsibility

The Pew Research Center surveyed Americans and asked if adults have a responsibility to provide financial help to their parents if they are in need. A large majority, 75 percent, said that adults do have a responsibility to take care of their parents financially. But just over half of the respondents, 52 percent, said that adults have a responsibility to help their grown children (over 18) if they are in need.

But many people find that the benefits of a multigenerational home far outweigh any of the little changes that are needed. Grandparents can help with child care, for one thing. Not only does that help out the family budget, but

Kids benefit from having attention from earlier generations of their families.

getting extra attention from loving adults is a benefit to the kids as well. Also, having everyone in the same place and knowing they are safe can greatly reduce the stress in a parent's life.

Text-Dependent Questions

1. Where did the term *sandwich families* come from?
2. According to the U.S. Census Bureau, how many of these families are there?
3. What are some of the benefits of this living arrangement?

Research Project

Although novels tell made-up stories, they can be an interesting way to learn about how different people view the world. Choose a novel from the suggestions below, or ask your teacher or librarian for another suggestion. As you read the book, take notes about the family relationships. Which family member is the main caregiver? Where do grandparents, aunts, or uncles live? What is their role in the family?

- *A Tree Grows in Brooklyn* by Betty Smith
- *Bud, Not Buddy* by Christopher Paul Curtis
- *Little House on the Prairie* by Laura Ingalls Wilder
- *Member of the Wedding* by Carson McCullers
- *Walk Two Moons* by Sharon Creech
- *The Witch of Blackbird Pond* by Elizabeth George Speare

More than 2 million grandparents have sole responsibility for looking after their grandkids.

Chapter Three

SKIPPED GENERATION FAMILIES

There's an old song you might have heard when you were little: "Over the river and through the wood, to grandmother's house we go." It's based on a poem that was written by Lydia Maria Child in the 1800s. (In her poem, she wrote "grandfather's house," but most people sing it as "grandmother.")

If you're lucky enough to have grandparents still living, you might think of their house as a favorite place to visit. Maybe you celebrate holidays there,

Words to Understand

custody: in this context, the legal right to make decisions for a child.

deportation: the act of sending someone who is not a citizen away.

fixed income: the same amount of money every month or year, with no expectation of increase.

grandfamilies: a term for families that are headed by a grandparent.

kinship: family relationship.

or maybe you go there for vacation. But for increasing numbers of kids, Grandmother's house is not just a place to visit: it's home.

AT GRANDMA'S TO STAY

Many parents look forward to the time when they'll become grandparents. This is because being a grandparent is said to have all the good parts of parenting (like playing with kids and giving presents) but none of the bad parts (like dealing with tantrums, discipline, and messes). Many grandparents comment that they love to spend short periods of time with their grandkids . . . and they also love giving the kids back at the end of the visit!

But life doesn't always work out the way we expect. Increasing numbers of grandparents are taking responsibility for their grandkids. These grandparents become, in effect, "parents" all over again—long after they thought that phase of their lives had ended. According to the support group Generations United, more than 2.5 million grandparents in the United States (that's 1 in 24) report that they are the main person responsible for looking after their grandkids. The official term for this is **kinship** *care*; kids in kinship care are raised by close family members. Kinship care is an alternative to foster care, where kids live with unrelated families or in group homes.

Sometimes these arrangements are temporary, but frequently they are long-term. Generations United reports that about 40 percent of grandparents who are raising their grandkids have been doing so for five years or more.

WHEN LIFE GETS COMPLICATED

There are many reasons why kids might end up living with their grandparents instead of their parents. They might stay with their grandparents for just a short while—for example, if a parent has to take a job out of state for a few months but then returns—or the kids might stay permanently. Just a few possible reasons for a permanent arrangement are:

- divorce and/or **custody** problems
- death of a parent
- incarceration of a parent
- military service
- job loss
- **deportation**
- drug or alcohol problems
- severe physical or mental illness

In times of crisis, grandparents sometimes find themselves taking care of babies for the first time in 20 or 30 years.

According to the most recent U.S. census, more than 2.4 million children are being raised by relatives rather than their parents. That's about 3 percent of kids in the entire United States. However, that number is a nationwide average—if you look at particular states, some have more kids in kinship care, while others have fewer. States with the highest numbers (about 6 percent of that state's kids) include Delaware, Kentucky, Louisiana, and West Virginia.

UP SIDES AND DOWN SIDES

You might be wondering, is it good or bad for kids to be raised by their grandparents? That's not an easy question to answer. And the truth is, there is no single answer that applies to all kids. There are good and bad aspects that might apply, depending on the specific situation.

Certainly, grandparents who are raising younger kids can face a lot of challenges. Most grandparents were not expecting to end up raising kids again later in life, which means they might not be prepared financially. Statistics show

Health care can be tricky for grandparents with kids, especially if legal custody is not entirely clear.

Case Study: Melody

There are many children being raised by their grandparents together, or by one of their grandmothers alone. Not so many being raised by their grandfathers alone. But that's what happened to Melody James.

"When my parents died in a car accident when I was baby," Melody says, "my grandfather stepped in. . . . If he hadn't, I don't know what would have happened to me. For as long as I can remember, he was my mother, father, and best friend, all rolled into one. He took care of me like it was the thing that made him the happiest in the world," Melody recalls. He was the most loving parent I have ever seen, and I consider myself to be tremendously lucky."

Melody's grandfather was already retired when she came to live with him, so he had plenty of time to devote to his young granddaughter. "He was always fixing something or volunteering to help someone with something, and he'd bring me along with him."

But her grandfather's retirement also meant he lived on a **fixed income**. "I didn't realize it at the time," Melody says, "but I see now that we didn't have much money. We ate a lot of macaroni and cheese and frozen dinners, and I didn't have as many toys as a lot of kids my age, and I never had all the clothes other little girls did. But I didn't really care. Those things never seemed all that important to me."

Melody believes that who she is today is largely due to her grandfather's influence on her life. "Grandpa was always there for me. . . . He helped me with my homework, played checkers with me after supper, took me out to lunch after church on Sundays. I loved being with him."

—Adapted from *Grandparents Raising Kids* by Rae Simons (Mason Crest, 2010)

that these grandparents tend to be poorer than their friends who aren't raising grandchildren. Almost a third of grandparents caring for kids live in poverty, and a full third have no health insurance. These grandparents are more than twice as likely to experience food insecurity, meaning that they lack dependable sources of food and sometimes go hungry.

Another challenge is that grandparents don't have an automatic legal right to make decisions for their grandkids. This can leave grandparents in a difficult situation. For example, if their grandchild needs medical care, or if a big decision needs to be made about school, the grandparents may not have the legal rights they need to be in charge of those decisions.

There can be other problems, too. Older people are more likely to have disabilities or other health problems, which can make it difficult for them to also be

There are downsides to being raised by grandparents, but there are a lot of benefits, too.

in charge of young kids. Grandparents may have to deal with feelings of grief, disappointment, or even anger that their adult children are not able to care for their own kids. Sometimes they feel separated from their friends who aren't raising kids and have fewer responsibilities.

But the news is not all bad, either. Kids who are in kinship care tend to do better than kids who are in foster care with strangers. They are more likely to stay connected with their brothers, sisters, and other extended family members, and this is associated with better outcomes later in life.

In addition to benefitting the grandchildren themselves, the existence of **grandfamilies** also helps society in general. The group Generations United estimates that keeping these kids out of the foster care system saves U.S. taxpayers $4 billion dollars every year. And while kids can be exhausting at times, many grandparents report that having kids around often gives them a renewed sense of purpose in life.

Text-Dependent Questions

1. Roughly how many grandparents in the United States are the main person in charge of their grandkids?
2. What are some of the potential problems for grandparents who are raising kids?
3. How much do these grandparents save taxpayers every year?

Research Project

Choose a particular family situation that is discussed in the course of this book, such as divorce or incarceration. Find out more about what advice experts give to kids in these situations. (See, for example, "Dealing with Divorce" on the KidsHealth website, at http://kidshealth.org/teen/your_mind/families/divorce.html.) Write a letter to an imaginary kid who is going through that situation. What advice can you give to help that kid cope?

Raising grandkids can involve a lot of forms and paperwork, so experts advise keeping everything together in one folder.

Chapter Four

MAKING IT WORK

Sometimes multigenerational families are created on purpose. As discussed in chapter two, it often just makes sense for extended families to move in together, so the family becomes multigenerational by choice. But other times, families become multigenerational by necessity. If a parent is sick, jailed, or some other situation comes up, grandparents may need to step in and take care of the kids. It can happen all of a sudden, and it can be a big shock sometimes.

Fortunately, there is lots of support available. This chapter collects some of the best advice for grandfamilies, and more can be found in the "Further Reading" section at the back of the book.

THE BASICS

As mentioned in chapter three, grandparents trying to get their grandkids to a doctor or registered for school can run into legal and custody questions. The

Words to Understand

social worker: a person whose job is to help families or children deal with particular problems.

subsidies: money that's given in order to assist someone with a particular job or activity.

organization AARP says that grandparents should gather up all the legal paperwork they can and keep it in a special folder. This might include birth certificates, social security numbers, marriage or divorce records, citizenship or adoption papers, records of child support payments, and any consent forms signed by the biological parents. Keeping all the paperwork in the same place sounds like a small thing, but it will be a big stress reliever if questions come up.

Grandparents might be surprised by just how many people they have to speak with when it comes to raising their grandkids. This can include **social workers** (both from the state and the local school), teachers, lawyers, and doctors. Grandparents should keep a notebook with information about all of these discussions: the name of the person, their job or relationship to the child, their contact information, the subject of the conversation, and any notes about what needs to happen as a result of the conversation. As with the documents folder, it seems like a small thing, but simply having everyone's contact information in one place will make life easier later on.

FINANCES

If you are a kid, you are expensive. It's not your fault, but you are. However, there are programs and services that provide financial assistance to kids and their grandparents. The National Council on Aging has an online survey (www.benefitscheckup.org) that can help older people figure out types of benefits they qualify for.

A federal law in 2008 called the Fostering Connections to Success and Increasing Adoptions Act made it easier for states to pay **subsidies** to people—frequently grandparents—who take care of kids. The exact rules vary by state, so guardians need to find out exactly how the program works where they live.

Sometimes grandparents who had retired decide that they need to go back to work in order to support their grandkids. Other grandparents are already working and find it can be challenging to balance both their jobs and their new responsibilities. AARP worked with the U.S. Department of Labor to create the

Being responsible for grandkids can bring a lot of expenses that grandparents were not necessarily expecting.

program Virtual Career Network (https://www.vcn.org/backtowork50plus). The Virtual Career Network is designed to help older people who want to reenter or stay in the job market.

All the grandkids—even the ones who aren't living with their grandparents—need to know that they are special, too.

GETTING ALONG

Whether a family is a "skipped generation" or a "sandwich" family, there are special challenges involved in blending different generations under the same roof. Here are some tips to make the transition easier:

- **Respect private space**. As much as possible, let each person in the house have a bit of their own space and a bit of time to themselves. If grandparents have been living on their own for a long time, it can be very challenging to suddenly have other people around. Giving people "their space" helps make them feel more secure. Depending on the particular house, this can be easy or hard. But even if you don't live in a big house where everyone has their own room, even small spaces—like having a favorite chair to watch TV or a clean place to do homework—can make a big difference.

- **Try to make a consistent schedule**. It's not easy, but try to have consistent meal times, bedtimes, and other rituals that you follow. This helps support a sense of normality in the house, which reduces stress.

- **Talk things over**. Try to make a regular "appointment" for all the family members to sit down, put away their phones, and talk about how things are going. This can help your family address small problems before they turn into big ones.

- **Don't forget the rest of your family**. When grandparents are living with or even raising some of their grandkids, it can have an effect on the *other* grandkids they aren't raising. Those kids might feel a little left out, or jealous of their siblings or cousins who get more attention from Grandma. If possible, these cousins should be included in special activities and get their own grandparent-time occasionally.

Text-Dependent Questions

1. What should grandparents put in the folders recommended by the AARP?
2. How can older people find out about what benefits they qualify for?
3. What are some tips to make daily life in a sandwich or skipped generation family easier?

Research Project

Create a pamphlet that has advice for skipped generation families. Start with the advice in this book, and then expand your research. You can try the websites mentioned in the text, for example. If your school has a counselor, interview that person to find out what programs or advice the school offers.

FURTHER READING

Books and Articles

Fry, Richard, and Jeffrey S. Passel. "In Post-Recession Era, Young Adults Drive Continuing Rise in Multigenerational Living." Pew Research Center. http://www.pewsocialtrends.org/2014/07/17/in-post-recession-era-young-adults-drive-continuing-rise-in-multi-generational-living/.

LaBan, Elizabeth. *The Grandparents' Handbook: Games, Activities, Tips, How-Tos, and All-Around Fun.* Philadelphia, PA: Quirk Books, 2009.

Online

AARP. "Grandparents Raising Grandchildren." http://www.aarp.org/relationships/friends-family/info-08-2011/grandfamilies-guide-getting-started.html.

Generations United. "Grandfamilies." http://www2.gu.org/OURWORK/Grandfamilies.aspx.

Generations United. "State of Grandfamilies in America: 2014." http://www.gu.org/RESOURCES/Publications/StateofGrandfamiliesinAmerica2014.aspx.

Grandfamilies of America. www.grandfamiliesofamerica.com.

Get Help Now

Childhelp National Child Abuse Hotline

This free hotline is available 24-hours-a-day in 170 different languages.

1-800-4-A-CHILD (1-800-422-4453)   http://www.childhelp.org

SERIES GLOSSARY

agencies: departments of a government with responsibilities for specific programs.

anxiety: a feeling of worry or nervousness.

biological parents: the woman and man who create a child; they may or not raise it.

caregiving: helping someone with their daily activities.

cognitive: having to do with thinking or understanding.

consensus: agreement among a particular group of people.

custody: legal guardianship of a child.

demographers: people who study information about people and communities.

depression: severe sadness or unhappiness that does not go away easily.

discrimination: singling out a group for unfair treatment.

disparity: a noticeable difference between two things.

diverse: having variety; for example, "ethnically diverse" means a group of people of many different ethnicities.

ethnicity: a group that has a shared cultural heritage.

extended family: the kind of family that includes members beyond just parents and children, such as aunts, uncles, cousins, and so on.

foster care: raising a child (usually temporarily) that is not adopted or biologically yours.

heir: someone who receives another person's wealth and social position after the other person dies.

homogenous: a group of things that are the same.

ideology: a set of ideas and ways of seeing the world.

incarceration: being confined in prison or jail.

inclusive: accepting of everyone.

informally: not official or legal.

institution: an established organization, custom, or tradition.

kinship: family relations.

neglect: not caring for something correctly.

patriarchal: a system that is run by men and fathers.

prejudice: beliefs about a person or group based only on simplified and often mistaken ideas.

prevalence: how common a particular trait is in a group of people.

psychological: having to do with the mind.

quantify: to count or measure objectively.

restrictions: limits on what someone can do.

reunification: putting something back together.

secular: nonreligious.

security: being free from danger.

social worker: a person whose job is to help families or children deal with particular problems.

socioeconomic: relating to both social factors (such as race and ethnicity) as well as financial factors (such as class).

sociologists: people who study human society and how it operates.

spectrum: range.

stability: the sense that things will stay the same.

stereotype: a simplified idea about a type of person that is not connected to actual individuals.

stigma: a judgment that something is bad or shameful.

stressor: a situation or event that causes upset (stress).

traumatic: something that's very disturbing and causes long-term damage to a person.

variable: something that can change.

INDEX

Page numbers in *italics* refer to photographs or tables.

ABOUT THE AUTHOR

H. W. Poole is a writer and editor of books for young people, including the 13-volume set, *Mental Illnesses and Disorders: Awareness and Understanding* (Mason Crest). She created the *Horrors of History* series (Charlesbridge) and the *Ecosystems* series (Facts On File). She has also been responsible for many critically acclaimed reference books, including *Political Handbook of the World* (CQ Press) and the *Encyclopedia of Terrorism* (SAGE). She was coauthor and editor of *The History of the Internet* (ABC-CLIO), which won the 2000 American Library Association RUSA award.

PHOTO CREDITS